'I will give you a new name.'

(Revelation 2:17)

Peter Walker
www.1peter1three.weebly.com

To you -
'the apple of God's eye.'

Introduction

I didn't choose to be born.

In other words, I didn't choose to exist. I didn't choose my parents or my circumstances. I definitely did not choose my looks or my personality. And yet these things and these people seem to define me.

I didn't choose for those bad things to happen. But they mark me. They made me fear, fight, be insecure, and even do things I wish I didn't do. And now these things seem to define me.

How do I get out of this maze?

Who am I *really*? Where do I belong?

God says, ***'I have loved you with an everlasting love,'*** and ***'before you were born I called you by name.'***[1]

In this short book we look at what God says about you, about me, and how we can find our way home…

---

[1] Jeremiah 1:5; 31:3

1. Family

'Though my father and mother forsake me, the Lord receives me.'
(Psalm 27:10)

For some of us the word and reality of 'father' makes us feel lost and less. For others, it is the only sense of being safe. Same goes for 'mother'.

Some people spend their lives looking for their father or their father's approval. Others spend their lives trying to shake the memory. Same goes for 'mother'.

Family here on earth is a complex, vulnerable reality. And yet none of us pick our parents. You get what you get. So why do we put so much store in who they are, and our relationship to them?

And did our earthly mother and father *actually* have that much to do with our existence? Seriously? They did something, but nothing very scientific or intentional. And then you were born!

Your parents can't 'create' you anymore than they can create a flower or a fly. No human has the power to create. And yet we feel our identity and destiny are tied to these people.

Look at what Jesus said to a crowd when his mother and siblings came looking for him, and were standing within earshot:

'Jesus said to the crowd, 'Who is my mother, and who are my brothers?' Pointing to his disciples, he said, 'Here are my mother and my brothers. For whoever does the will of my Father in heaven is my brother and sister and mother."
(Matthew 12:48-50)

The truth is we all have only one Creator, one *true* Father. All of us! We are told that God in heaven is the one from whom every 'father' gets his title.[1]

This Father we actually *can* choose. He created us, loves us, but allows us to choose him back. Or not.

---

[1] Ephesians 3:14-15

We can't choose our earthly parents, but we *can* choose God as our true, perfect Father.

'Jesus came to that which was his own, but his own did not receive him. Yet <u>to all who did receive him, to those who believed in his name, he gave the right to become children of God</u> - children born not of natural descent, nor of human decision, but born of God.' (John 1:11-13)

2. True Light

'The people walking in darkness have seen a great light.' (Isaiah 9:2)

It's interesting how things change when the sun goes down.

During the light of day everyone seems so full of strong opinions. But then the night settles in. People get weak and fade. Everything goes quiet, and everything goes dark. Our views on life, our confidence, even arrogance, slips away.

The *truth* about you, about me, can't change like shifting shadows. Or it's not truth. God's truth about you, about me, is rock solid when the sun is high or the sun is hiding.

'Even the darkness will not be dark to you, Lord. The night will shine like the day, for darkness is as light to you.' (Psalm 139:12)

Jesus was referred to as the ***'true light'***. He is ***'God with us'***.[1]

---

[1] John 1:9; Matthew 1:23/Isaiah 7:14

Jesus created the Day, and he created the Darkness. He owns it all. In God all darkness is holy, restful, a type of covering and peace. It has no evil in it, no doubt or insecurity.

When we step into the true light of Jesus, we step into a place of true belonging.

In Christ you come back to the very source of your soul, his *'true light'* shines on the *'true you.'*

'On those living in the land of deep darkness a light has dawned.'
(Isaiah 9:2b)

3. Your True Name

'Jesus said, 'To the one who is victorious I will give a white stone with a new name written on it, known only to the one who receives it."
(Revelation 2:17)

Here Jesus is speaking to a church. They are going through hard times, living in a city where their faith in Jesus is not accepted, a place where Jesus himself said *'Satan has his throne.'* One member of this church, Antipas, was put to death for his faith.

Jesus speaks to them and calls them to hold on tight, to continue in their faith. He also tells them to repent of their sin. Even these people, under pressure and persecution, Jesus expects to turn away from their wrongdoing.

Then he gives them this promise. It feels sublime to me, ethereal: To the one who is victorious – stays true to Jesus – they will be given a new name, a secret name, written on a white stone.

This new name, true name, comes at the end of a life of faith in Christ. It comes at the end of the journey, and bears the mark of our 'victory', our walk with God. This name – your truest name – is in the hand of God and will be given you when you cross life's finish line, faithful in Jesus.

****

When I was a kid I wasn't crazy about my name, 'Peter'. I know my parents gave me this biblical name with intention, with a sense of significance. But as a kid it sounded kinda heavy to me, or boring.

Skip ahead a few years, and I distinctly remember the time my wife and I – and the midwife! – were discussing what name to put on my daughter's birthcert. We had a couple names we liked, not sure of the order, maybe Rachel Anna, or Anna Rachel… We made a decision, put it on the form, and got on with life. Simpe as that.

So what really is in a name here on earth? Well, not much. A name is a 'sound' to get your attention. Now, what people associate with your name will depend on what they associate with your character. But the title itself, the 'word', is something other people picked and stuck on you. It works for this life, for coding, for calling, etc. But it has no inherent meaning.

The name God gives you when you cross the river, when you walk through his gates, well, that's a different name. It is spiritual, it is deep and even secret, and it will have in its very 'sound', so to speak, the victory of your faith – and faithfulness – here on earth.

This will be your true name. It's up ahead. But even now, your faith in God, your walk with his Son, Jesus Christ, is what will determine this name.

4. Who Are You?

'Many people believed in Jesus. But Jesus would not entrust himself to them, for he knew all people... He knew what was in each person.'
(John 2:22-24)

This is a lonely life. The world is a dangerous place. From a very young age we look to be in groups, just to feel safe. The truth is, however, we usually want to be in a group of people to be safe from another group of people. People are the problem. I am the problem.

Even when Jesus was being approved of, *'many people believing'*, he did not *'entrust himself to them.'* Jesus knows the heart of people. His mission here was to save us from our sin, from ourselves, he didn't come to get our approval. He doesn't need our following, our support or our protection.

And the truth is we don't need the support, following or protection of other people when it comes to our decision to follow Jesus. If you entrust yourself to Jesus, and not to the crowd, well, you stand with the King of the world, the Judge of all humanity. You are safe here.

And Jesus calls us to be faithful, to be true, to this relationship with him. To put him above all else, all others, even our own desires. And where any other loyalty competes with this, Jesus calls us to lay that one down and follow him.

Look carefully at this passage:

'As they were walking along the road, a man said to Jesus, "I will follow you wherever you go."

Jesus replied, "Foxes have dens and birds have nests, but the Son of Man has no place to lay his head."

Jesus said to another man, "Follow me." But he replied, "Lord, first let me go and bury my father."

Jesus said to him, "Let the dead bury their own dead, but you go and proclaim the kingdom of God."

Still another said, "I will follow you, Lord; but first let me go back and say goodbye to my family."

Jesus replied, "No one who puts a hand to the plow and looks back is fit for service in the kingdom of God."

(Luke 9:57-62)

We are told that Jesus came to save us from our sin. (Matthew 1:21) Simple as that. He called us to repent, which means to turn away from sin in our life. In this respect, Jesus actually came to get us *out* of groups, not into them.

Many of the groups we join – *fraternities, sororities, clubs, organizations, political parties* – compete with the spiritual family we have joined in Jesus. They often have a call to a type of loyalty to people, which in itself can be dangerous. Because very soon, as a 'member' of this or that group, you may be asked to compromise your morals or your values in order to be loyal to another member. And so you are disloyal to God in order to be loyal to this group.

For this reason, despite approval and praise, Jesus would not *'entrust himself'* to people. He would not join a group.

When we commit ourselves to Jesus Christ, we have joined ourselves to God himself. Nothing can compete with this.

'Then Jesus called the crowd to him and said: "Whoever wants to be my disciple must deny themselves and take up their cross and follow me. Whoever wants to save their life will lose it, but whoever loses their life for me and for the gospel will save it. What good is it for someone to gain the whole world, yet forfeit their soul? Or what can anyone give in exchange for their soul? If anyone is ashamed of me and my words in this adulterous and sinful generation, I will be ashamed of them when I come in my Father's glory with the holy angels."

(Mark 8:34-38)

5. What Is the Gospel?

We just read above that Jesus said, **'Whoever loses their life for me and for the gospel will save it.'** (Mark 8:35)

The word 'gospel' just means *'good news.'*

Jesus himself *is* the gospel, the *'good news.'*

The Bible clearly teaches that Jesus is God in the flesh. He is referred to as God's Son, with the meaning that God stepped down into the form of man, in order to see us, touch us, love us and save us. Jesus is **'God with us.'** (Matthew 1:23)

'Jesus, in his very nature God, made himself nothing and became a man.' (Philippians 2:6-7)

When Jesus came and met with us, holy and true, he called us to turn away from sin in our lives, and come to him. When we turn away from sin (repent) and come to Jesus in belief (faith), we are saved. We are safe. We belong.

Now, although Jesus is the 'good news', it is important to know what he actually did for us when he was here on earth. He had a very deep, spiritual mission.

Through the prophets God had always taught us that the penalty for sin was death. For this reason religious people would sacrifice animals as a payment for their sin. This was the command of God, and it was deeply symbolic.

Then the time came when Jesus – God himself – would be the ultimate sacrifice for our sin. He was holy and true, and was referred to as the ***'Lamb of God who takes away the sin of the world.'*** (John 1:29)

Lambs were sacrificed for sin, which you can read about all through the first half of the Bible. But then Jesus came, and he *was* the ultimate lamb, the ultimate sacrifice. When Jesus died on the cross, he was dying for our sin. He was the sacrifice for our sin.

Then when he rose again from the dead, he stretched out his hand and offered us forgiveness for sin. The forgiveness he had just earned us by paying for our sin.

'The death Jesus died, he died to sin once for all.' (Romans 6:10)

Jesus is the gospel, the 'good news.' His death on the cross paid for our sin. He now calls us to himself.

'Anyone who is in Christ is a new creation. The old has gone, the new has come.' (2 Corinthians 5:17)

6. <u>Stepping In</u>

'Jesus said, 'I am the door. Anyone who comes through me will be saved, and he will go in and come out and find pasture.'' (John 10:9)

Jesus called people to follow him. Now, not everyone could actually go with him everywhere he went. In fact, one man asked to and Jesus declined, telling him to go back to his village and share with others about Jesus. In this man's life following Jesus meant going the other way, going home.

So what did Jesus really mean by *'follow'*? Well, he meant – and often said – to believe in him. He called people to turn away from wrong in their life, from 'sin', and to believe in him as God and Savior.

Jesus would do miracles to show people his power, in order to prove to people that he was God. One time he even said openly that he was doing a miracle so that people would know he could forgive sin.[1]

---

[1] Luke 5:20,24

When the people asked Jesus what *'the work of God'* was, he answered:

'The work of God is this, to believe in me, the one he has sent.' (John 6:29)

Again, he said:

'My Father's will is that everyone who looks to me and believes in me will have eternal life, and I will raise them up on the last day.' (John 6:40)

Even though Jesus is no longer here on earth physically, he is here by his Spirit. He said that when he left he would pour out his Spirit on the earth. We can still speak with him, and come to him.[1]

A beautiful way to step through the door of Jesus, to come to him, is through prayer.

If you have made a decision to turn away from your sin, and receive Jesus into your life, you can pray this prayer right now. Simply read it, but in your heart and spirit be speaking it to Jesus:

---

[1] John 16:7-16

Dear Jesus, I believe in you. I come to you. I want to belong to God.

Jesus, I am sorry for the sin in my life. I want to turn away from it now and go your way, walk on your path. Please help me to do this!

Thank you for coming to this world, for dying to pay for my sin, and for saving me now.

I love you. I receive you. Thank you! Amen.

7. **You Belong!**

If you have believed in Jesus, and received his forgiveness and Spirit, you are saved. You are a child of God. You belong.

Look at this incredible verse:

'Once you were not a people, but now you are the people of God. Once you had not received mercy, but now you have received mercy.' (1 Peter 2:10)

Your truest name lay ahead, and will be bestowed on you, as we read from Revelation 2:17: ***'To those who are victorious I will give a new name written on a white stone…'***

You belong to the family of God, in Jesus Christ. And you are not just a member of a family, but a *unique* creation of God – a son, a daughter, with a secret name on the heart of God, and one day written on your very own white stone. Even now you are unique, set apart, loved.

'Anyone who is in Christ is a new creation. The old has gone, the new has come!' (2 Corinthians 5:17)

Thank you for taking time to read this book!

If you are just starting your new life with Jesus, please read the book called, 'First Steps With Jesus', free on the website and the APP (1Peter1:3):

www.1peter1three.weebly.com

***'Keep me as the apple of your eye;
hide me in the shadow of your
wings.'*** (Psalm 17:8)

*(a simple prayer that you can whisper,
because you are the apple of God's eye!)*

Made in the USA
Columbia, SC
20 November 2024